ABUSE IS A VERB

How to talk and write about abuse

Natalie Collins

First published in Great Britain in 2024.

The Women's Liberation Collective
The Co-op Centre
Sunderland, SR2 8AH

Copyright © Natalie Collins 2017

All rights reserved. No part of this book may be reproduced in any form, stored in a retrieval system, or transmitted in any form, by any means - electronic, mechanical, photocopy, recording or otherwise - without prior permission of the publisher, except as provided by UK copyright law.

The author has made every effort to ensure that the external website and email addresses included in this book are correct and up to date at the time of going to press. The author is not responsible for the content, quality, or continuing accessibility of the sites.

Contact the author: info@ownmylifecourse.org

For further resources to understand abuse please visit:
www.ownmylifediscovery.org.

This book is dedicated to Jo Costello, who is such a brilliant cheerleader; she is the best woman I know.

Contents

Introduction 1

Definitions 3

Part 1: Us 7

Part 2: Him 29

Part 3: Her 55

Part 4 : Notes 87

Recommended Reading 89

Bibliography 90

Introduction

"Words create worlds."[1]
Judith E. Glaser

Our words shape the world and our understanding of it. This book is not designed to fully qualify you in understanding abuse perpetrated within a relationship (often described as domestic abuse). There are plenty of books that can do this, some of these (including my previous book) are listed on page 95. For more interactive resources, you could join Own My Life Discovery, which has CPD accredited videos and activities to help you understand abuse and trauma: www.ownmylifediscovery.org. This book won't tell you everything about abuse, but it will help you to think about the language you use and enable you to communicate about abuse more effectively.

Abuse should be understood as a verb. It is something one person does to another. It is not a noun (as in, "the abuse she suffered"). In failing to talk and write about abuse as an action taken by a person we can collude with the abuser's desire to avoid responsibility and erase himself from the situation. Alongside this, abuse is very often euphemised and the words we use can (often unintentionally) reinforce myths and misunderstandings about abuse.

---

[1] Stockdale, 2016, 12.

Our language can domesticate abuse, making it less offensive and more palatable. Abuse should always be offensive. Abuse perpetrated within the home should be *more* horrific to us; when the home is not a safe place, humanity can never truly flourish.

To communicate competently about abuse does not require being an expert. Whether you are a professional working in the domestic abuse "sector", a journalist, an educator or a generally interested individual, this book should help you to articulate the issues more effectively. It is descriptive rather than prescriptive. While helpful and unhelpful examples are given, these are to aid understanding rather than insisted as the only wording ever allowed.

No one can stop abuse: except abusers. Our job is to plant seeds which challenge abusers, and challenges a wider society that too often colludes with those abusers. These seeds could grow into awareness in the minds and hearts of those subjected to abuse. They could grow into cultural opposition to abusive attitudes and beliefs. The words we use and the language we employ are part of planting those seeds. We can't immediately change the world, but by planting seeds in hearts and minds, we can gradually see change. Each page is titled with a word or phrase that is commonly used to communicate about abuse perpetrated within a relationship. There is then a brief explanation about why this is not helpful and examples are then provided of how (and how not) to talk about abuse.

Definitions

The current UK domestic abuse definition is:

Any incident or pattern of incidents of controlling, coercive or threatening behaviour, violence or abuse between those aged 16 or over who are or have been intimate partners or family members regardless of gender or sexuality. This can encompass but is not limited to the following types of abuse: Psychological, Physical, Sexual, Financial, Emotional.

Controlling behaviour is: a range of acts designed to make a person subordinate and/or dependent by isolating them from sources of support, exploiting their resources and capacities for personal gain, depriving them of the means needed for independence, resistance and escape and regulating their everyday behaviour. Coercive behaviour is: an act or a pattern of acts of assault, threats, humiliation and intimidation or other abuse that is used to harm, punish, or frighten their victim.
This definition, which is not a legal definition, includes so called 'honour' based violence, female genital mutilation (FGM) and forced marriage, and is clear that victims are not confined to one gender or ethnic group.[2]

---

[2] UK Government, 2022.

The language used within this definition is problematic:
1. Incidents of abuse do not happen "between" people, they happen from one person to another person. Abuse involves one person seeking power over and control of another. This doesn't happen reciprocally.
2. Abuse can be perpetrated by people who are under 16 years old, just as those who are under 16 can be subjected to abuse.
3. Although the definition is correct in saying that victims are not confined to one gender, it is important to acknowledge that domestic abuse perpetration is a gendered issue and should be treated as such. To solve a problem, we must understand it, and denying the gendered roots of abuse is to misunderstand why abuse is perpetrated.[3]
4. Although the concepts of abuse are labelled accurately as "Psychological, Physical, Sexual, Financial, Emotional", these are often used euphemistically. "Psychological abuse" is more palatable than articulating "my partner hides my keys so I think I'm going mad, he undermines my relationships with my friends and tracks my phone so that he knows where I am all the time. He mocks me when I share my ambitions and prevents me from sleeping by wanting to talk about his issues in the middle of the night. If I try to talk to him about this, he always manipulates me into thinking it's my fault". Conceptual labels for abuse are often

---

[3] Stark, 2009, 5, 15.

useful for brevity, but it is important that in using them we do not obscure the reality of abuse.

5. Although child sexual exploitation is not included within this definition, the perpetration of exploitation (of children and adults) will generally utilise the same methods to abuse and control. As such, this book is useful in rethinking communication about sexual exploitation. While it is limited to talking primarily about domestic abuse perpetrated within intimate relationships, it may also be useful for talking about the other categories of abuse listed within the definition, (e.g. female genital mutilation and force marriage).

Part 1: Us

Domestic Abuse.

Using the label "domestic abuse" or "domestic violence" to describe a perpetrator's choice to subject their partner to violence and abuse can lead to the perpetrator, as the agent of the abuse, being erased.

Unhelpful	Helpful
Some women are killed by domestic abuse.	Some women are killed by their partner or ex-partner.
Domestic violence damages children.	Children are damaged when one of their parents is abusing the other.
Domestic abuse is a blight upon society.	The choice of some people to abuse, control and hurt their partner damages society as a whole.

Abusive Relationship.

Using the term "abusive relationship" makes the abuse a relationship issue, rather than an abuser's issue.[4] It infers that the problem is relationship issues and that relationship solutions will help. It also suggests that when the relationship ends, the abuse will end. This is rarely the case with male perpetrators as they will often perpetrate post-separation abuse. Overall, the term "abusive relationship" reinforces myths about abuse and erases the perpetrator's responsibility and agency.

Unhelpful	Helpful
She finally escaped her abusive relationship.	She finally left her abusive partner.
It was a really bad abusive relationship.	He was a really abusive partner.
We need to respond to the issue of abusive relationships.	We need to respond to the issue of people choosing to behave in abusive and controlling ways.

---

[4] Okun, 1986, pp. xx-xxi. Collins, 2019, pp.40-41.

It Happened.

Rain happens. Illness happens. Abuse does not "happen". It is a choice made by one person to control and abuse another person. The abuser will generally make this choice because they believe they are entitled to do what they want. Often their abusive behaviour will benefit them; their behaviour will lead to the abuser's partner (and any children) becoming compliant, blaming themselves, and doing as they are told. By saying the abuse "happened", we erase the perpetrator's agency and infer that the abuse is a one-off event. Abuse is a pattern of behaviour. It includes the ongoing traumatic impact of the abuser's behaviour that can continue long after someone escapes the abuser.[1]

Unhelpful	Helpful
I'm sorry that happened to you.	I'm sorry that was done to you.
He experienced abuse.	He was subjected to abuse.
She suffered abuse.	She was subjected to abuse.

1 in 4 women and 1 in 6 men will be abused.

This statistic is often quoted to evidence almost equal perpetration of abuse by men and women. However this is misleading comparison. Professor Marianne Hester's 2009 study, based on police reports, and accounting for the dynamics of domestic violence, found that 5% of domestic violence incidents were perpetrated by women in heterosexual relationships.[5] This aligns with the ONS data that 92% of defendants in domestic abuse related crime are male.[6]

Unhelpful	Helpful
Domestic abuse can affect anyone.	Anyone can choose to behave abusively, however the majority of abusers are male and the majority of those they abuse are female.
Yes, abuse can happen anywhere, but it's worse in other countries.	Abuse is perpetrated in every country. We mustn't use abuse in other places to minimise what abusers do in our country/community.

---

[5] Hester, 2009.
[6] ONS, 2016.

A domestic.

Within policing there has been a culture of devaluing abuse perpetrated within a relationship. Historically "it's just a domestic" has been used to ignore serious crime. Although in many police forces this has stopped, there continues to be a culture of treating crimes committed within the context of a relationship (even if the relationship has formally ended) in a different way to other crime. Part of this is practical; crimes committed within the domestic sphere usually involve a known perpetrator and certain patterns of behaviour, however crimes committed towards a partner or ex-partner are not categorised differently under law. Assault is still assault, criminal damage is still criminal damage, murder is still murder. Prioritising the term "domestic" above the crime that has been committed reinforces unhelpful attitudes and beliefs about abuse and abusers. While Coercive Control is now a criminal offence, it is important that appropriate legal terms are used for all offences.

Unhelpful	Helpful
It's a domestic.	It's a report of assault, the suspected perpetrator is the victim's ex-partner.
I'm responding to a domestic.	I'm responding to a report of a woman having been shot. The perpetrator may be known to the victim.

Isolated incident.

Police media statements often describe crimes perpetrated towards a partner or family member as an "isolated incident". The intention in doing this is to convey that there is no wider risk to the public. It creates the perception that this is the sole incident involving the suspect and victim, when in reality criminal acts perpetrated within a relationship are almost always part of a wider campaign of controlling and abusive behaviour. Another (perhaps) unintended consequence of this is that the structural nature of abusive behaviour is ignored. Male violence against women remains at epidemic proportions. 1425 women were killed by men in the UK between 2008 – 2018,[7] with perpetration of domestic abuse costing the UK economy nearly £19 billion every year.[8] The human cost of abusers' choices is astronomical and horrific. To describe each incident that is considered "newsworthy" as isolated embeds within public consciousness that these crimes are not a structural issue happening nationally (and globally). It allows us to distance those type incidents and make them something unrelated to everyday life. Those "isolated incidents" are happening up and down the country, perpetrated towards our neighbours, friends, family members and colleagues.

Unhelpful	Helpful
This murder is an isolated incident.	We've identified those involved in this case and are not looking for other suspects.

---

[7] Long, Wertans, et al., 2019.
[8] Oliver, Alexander et al., 2019.

Revenge porn.

In 2015, it became illegal in the UK to disclose "private sexual photographs or films without the consent of an individual who appears in them and with intent to cause that individual distress".[9] While it is technically correct to describe this offence as "revenge porn", such terminology is harmful. Pornography is the creation of content that "elicits sexual desire". Illegally sharing sexual images of a partner without their consent is not primarily about eliciting sexual desire but is rather about violation, degradation and control. A more appropriate term for this offence is "image-based sexual abuse". By describing this non-consensual disclosure of images as sexual abuse, it emphasises the harm it causes and ensures those who have been abused in this way are considered to have been abused. Similarly, using the term "child pornography" continues harmful myths about child sexual abuse, and is inaccurate. The correct term for sexual images of children is "child sexual abuse images".

Unhelpful	Helpful
She was a victim of revenge porn.	Her partner sexually abused her by sharing sexual images of her with others.
He threatened her with revenge porn.	He threatened to abuse her sexually by sending her parent sexual images of her.
They found child porn on his computer.	They found images of children being sexually abused on his computer.

---

[9] CPS, 2022.

Real men don't hit women.

The ideal of the "real man" props up abusive behaviour. As Audre Lorde explains, "The Master's Tools Will Never Dismantle the Master's House".[10] This is never going to work and masculine norms (in fact the entire concept of masculinity) contributes to a culture in which men choose to abuse women and other men. Masculinity presents itself as devoid of anything feminine; it is strong, powerful and virile.[11] Women become so different, so "other" that men don't have to treat them equally. Appealing to "real manhood" insists that there is something innate to men that is not in women. Rather than using "masculinity shaming" to stop men behaving abusively, it is of greater value to work to abolish masculinity (just as femininity) and in its place, perhaps we can each be human beings, working to make the world a better place? Alongside this, the focus on specific types of physical violence (in this instance "hitting women") allows men to absolve themselves. They may never have hit a woman, even though they have strangled, lied to, manipulated or isolated a woman.

Unhelpful	Helpful
Real men don't hurt women.	Many men do hurt women, and we need to address this.
Real men do cry.	Manhood insists boys shouldn't cry, we need to dismantle that and give males a sense of their full humanity, not just their masculinity.

---

[10] Lorde, 1984.
[11] Porter, 2010. Gelfer, 2011.

It's personal not political.

Rape and abuse do not exist in a vacuum. Perpetrators exist within a society where their behaviour is simultaneously abhorred and accepted. The pornification and objectification of women and girls in the media normalises abusive behaviour.[12] Gender inequality in business, law, media, politics and society privileges men and disadvantages women. This is the water in which we swim and we don't even notice that we're soaking wet. It's important we have a structural analysis when responding to any facet of male violence,* so that we are able to shape it within the wider context of our lives, our society and across the world.

Unhelpful	Helpful
Rape is a terrible thing to do; I have no idea why anyone would do it.	Men are constantly told they have rights over women's bodies and are entitled to get what they want from women, a logical consequence of this is that some men will rape women.
Pornography is hurting men and stopping them having fulfilling relationships.	When men masturbate whilst watching women being sexually degraded this damages their view of women and their capacity to have healthy relationships, whilst contributing to an industry that abuses women
We need to rescue people from sex trafficking.	We must work to abolish the sex industry and address the issues of poverty, abuse and oppression which cause women to enter the industry.

---

[12] Dines, 2010. French, 1992.

We can end domestic abuse.

We cannot *end* domestic abuse, but we can seek to stop the perpetration of abuse.[13] Although working to "end abuse" is a laudable goal; abuse will only end when people (mostly men) choose to stop being abusive. It can often be assumed that working to address the impact of abusers' behaviour can take place in isolation from dealing with other types of male violence. It cannot. Abusers choose abuse because they live within in a society (as we all do) where women are dehumanised and devalued, so much so that abusers think it is okay to treat them in whatever ways they want. Abuse perpetrated within a relationship is one branch of a much larger tree. We cannot seek to address it without also understanding the other parts of the tree; the objectification of women, unfair laws, unequal pay, gender stereotyping, pornography, trafficking, female genital mutilation, lack of representation of women in public spaces. The list goes on and on. Often certain branches on the tree can be seen as irrelevant or as "political correctness gone mad", but it is only in working to uproot the tree that we can really hope to end male violence.

Unhelpful	Helpful
Together we can end domestic abuse.	Together we can create a culture where abusive behaviour is not tolerated.
We will end abuse.	We will challenge abusive attitudes wherever we encounter them.

---

[13] Collins, 2019, 248-258. Bancroft, 2002, 367-389.

Part 2: Him

Abuse happens because...

When talking about abuse we may be under the misapprehension that those who choose to abuse others do so because of drug or alcohol issues,[14] stress, insecurity, mental or physical ill health, infidelity, anger issues, being on the autistic spectrum, a lack of healthy communication skills or childhood trauma. The abuser behaves abusively because it allows them to get what they want and because they believe their partner is less important than they are. Abusive behaviour is rooted in the abuser's beliefs of ownership and entitlement.[15]

Unhelpful	Helpful
He killed his wife and children because he couldn't bear to live without them.	He killed his wife and children because he believed he owned them.
Depression makes you do terrible things, that's why he was abusive.	Depression doesn't make people abusive. He chose to be abusive to his partner, yet chose not to be abusive to his boss.
He was so angry he pushed her.	Though he was angry, he chose to push her rather than punch her in the face. If he could choose how to hurt her, he could choose not to hurt her.
He abused her because he was insecure.	He abused her because he felt entitled to get what he wanted.

---

[14] Bodnàr, Nagy, Cziboly et al, 2021.
[15] Bancroft, 2002, 49-75. Collins, 2019, 39-63.

Unless.

"Abuse is always wrong, unless she cheated on him." "You should never hit a woman, unless…" While most people would agree that abusive behaviour is wrong, many of us hold onto "unlesses" which we believe reduces the culpability of the perpetrator. Each culture has its own unlesses, and we will likely view other culture's unlesses as barbaric, while being oblivious to the existence of our own. Within western culture, we might see that abuse is always wrong: unless she's had an affair; unless she tried to leave him; unless he's angry; unless she was out late and was drunk and was wearing skimpy clothing and was asking for it. For other cultures, the unlesses may include: unless she cooked the dinner badly; unless she answered back; unless she marries someone she chose for herself. We need to become aware of our unlesses and eradicate them from our culture, whichever culture that happens to be.[16]

Unhelpful	Helpful
It's terrible that he killed his children, but his wife had left him and he was scared he'd never see his children again.	It's barbaric that he killed his children.
Of course, he shouldn't have hit her, but he'd found out she was having an affair.	Of course he shouldn't have hit her.
Okay, so he shouldn't have done that, but she winds him up. I think I'd lose it if I had to live with her.	Okay, so he shouldn't have done that.

---

[16] Collins, 2019, 56-57.

But he's such a nice man.

When a woman tells us that someone we know has subjected them to abuse this can leave us shocked. We would never have suspected that they could behave in such terrible ways. By inferring that we didn't think the person would be abusive, we may communicate disbelief, reinforce the perpetrator's power, and perpetuate a "monster mentality" in which abusers are easily identifiable based on how they look or act. In reality, most abusers use their charm and emotional literacy to manipulate not just their partner, but everyone around them.

Unhelpful	Helpful
I can't believe he did that, he's such a nice man!	It's terrible that he's treated you this way and misled everyone into thinking he's a "nice guy".
Surely you must be mistaken?! He wouldn't do something like that.	It's terrible that he treated you this way.

Anger management.

It is a common misconception that abusive behaviour is rooted in anger issues. Abusive behaviour is not about anger, it's about control. Anger management resources often enable abusers to control their behaviour even further and can actually benefit the abuser. Which is why anger management classes or better communication skills are ineffective, and can even be dangerous. Abusive behaviour enables the abuser to get what they want. That's why they continue to use it. They may appear angry and (especially in western culture) the abuser may learn that appearing angry will more easily enable him to get away with his behaviour. We must stop talking about anger, anger issues or anger management in relation to abusive behaviour. Abusers do not need better communication skills; most are able to competently communicate with their colleagues, family and friends. It is solely with their intimate partner (and any children) that they use abusive behaviour.

Unhelpful	Helpful
He just lost it and started hitting her.	He started hitting her.
Most abusers have anger issues.	Most abusers have chosen to behave abusively.
Anger management is a useful intervention for perpetrators of abuse.	Anger management is not a useful intervention for perpetrators of abuse.

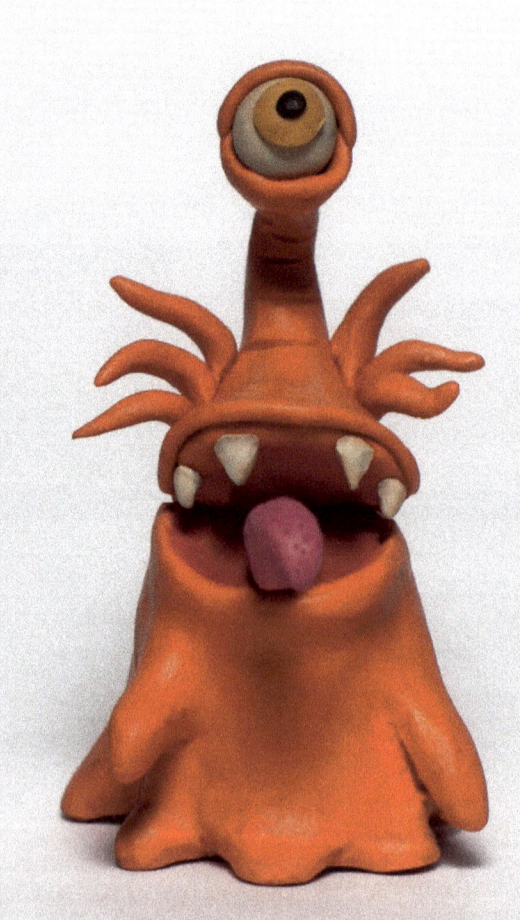

All abusers are…

Believing that all abusers are the same misunderstands the nature of abuse. All abusers may exhibit similar behaviours but there is no specific type of person who is abusive. Some abusers are very wealthy and some are very poor, some are highly educated while others are not. Some have high powered careers whereas others are in low paid jobs. Some struggle with substance misuse, many do not. The idea that only a certain type of person is abusive can leave us vulnerable to not noticing abusers around us, until it is too late. If he doesn't fit our "abuser profile" we may ignore warning signs and inappropriate behaviour because we're primed to assume he can't be an abuser. With the partners of our friends, family members and work colleagues, this may prevent us from offering them helpful advice and support.

Unhelpful	Helpful
No abuser is interested in politics.	An abusive person is no more or less likely to be interested in politics than anyone else, because abusers are part of the general public.
He can't be an abuser I would be able to tell.	He could be an abuser I wouldn't be able to tell.
He doesn't look like he's abusive.	It's impossible to identify an abuser solely by how he looks.

Jealousy.

There can be a presumption that an abuser's behaviour is motivated by jealousy. However, jealousy is a general human emotion. The abuser's belief of ownership towards his partner (and any children) means that rather than being motivated by jealousy, an abuser's behaviour is about possessiveness. He sees his partner as a possession that he is entitled to do what he wants with.

Unhelpful	Helpful
He gets really jealous of other men being around his partner.	He is very possessive.
It's understandable that he's jealous. We've all been there.	His possessiveness is unacceptable. His partner isn't his possession!

Redemption.

We all want a happy ending! And many of us want to believe that with the right support and help an abuser will change. We assume the abuser is a tortured soul; perhaps he has terrible trauma that drives him to be abusive? While all abusers have the potential to change, the benefits of abusive behaviour and a culture which leaves them unchallenged, means that most abusers don't change. We must be careful that our hope that abusers can change or be redeemed doesn't lead us to collude with him, minimise the harm he has caused, or leave us prioritising the abuser over those he is hurting.

Unhelpful	Helpful
Let's have a reformed perpetrator speaking at our event.	Let's invite a skilled person who works with perpetrators to bring a perspective on perpetrator work.
You can't access healing unless you forgive him for what he's done.	Forgiveness is a choice. You need to heal in the way that is most helpful to you.
He's really sorry and was so upset. I think he's really changed, maybe you should give him another chance.	Even if he's really upset, his behaviour may make it impossible to repair the relationship.

He's a {insert swearword here}.

When someone discloses to us what their partner has been doing to them, we may feel appalled. Our first response may be anger and to call the abuser bad names. However, if the relationship is still ongoing we need to maintain a relationship with the person discloses, not alienate them by being negative about their partner. The abuser will be attempting to isolate their partner and if we speak badly of him, this may work in his favour, evidencing that we are trying to sabotage the relationship. Rather than badmouthing the abuser, we can question the abuser's intentions. If the relationship has ended, our anger will rarely help the person who has been subjected to abuse. It may leave them feeling out of control, uncomfortable or like they are to blame for explaining the situation badly.

Unhelpful	Helpful
He's such a {insert swearword} for hiding your phone.	When he hid your phone, do you think his intention may have been to stop you contacting people? I'm not saying it was, but could it have been?
Right, I'm going to go round there to punch him.	Maybe he'll tell you that I'm out to get you or that I'm jealous of you or that I'm not a good friend, but I really love you and I am your friend and I'm here for you.
Why do you keep going back to him when he's so awful?	I know it's really hard and that it feels like he loves you. Maybe he keeps doing this because he knows he'll get away with it…

Special Occasions.

Many abusers escalate their behaviour during special occasions, especially cultural or religious festivals, or important occasions like birthdays, anniversaries, or funerals. There can be an assumption that this is due to financial pressures, stress, or (where relevant) increased alcohol consumption. However, these events are a trigger point because abusers deliberately seek to destroy moments that are precious to their partner and children in order to prove and maintain their control. At these times, an abuser's actions will have a greater impact. His partner may also be more compliant over a special occasion as she wants it to remain a positive and joyful time. In addition to this, the abuser and his partner may both be off work, with more spare time, which ensures greater opportunity for him to behave in abusive and controlling ways.

Unhelpful	Helpful
There is increased abuse at Christmas because it's a stressful time.	There is increased perpetration of abuse at Christmas because it's a special time.
Over special occasions, women are more likely to nag, which is why abuse happens more.	Over special occasions, abusers are more likely to be abusive because they want to destroy precious moments and prove they have all powere and control.

He's insecure.

When someone is abusive, it is often suggested that the problem is because the abuser is insecure. Their abusive behaviour may appear to be a form of jealousy, with an assumption that the jealousy is a by-product of insecurity. Some people may think, "He feels powerless in other areas of his life and so he wants to feel more powerful in his relationship."

This is not borne out in research about abuse.[17] Far from abusers being insecure, their abusive behaviour is rooted in a belief of being superior to their partner and a belief that the abuser owns his partner (and children) and is entitled to do what he wants to her. Such beliefs result in possessive behaviour. Counselling will not help an abuser to stop being abusive. Counselling looks at, "my feelings and other people's actions". An abuser needs to focus on, "other people's feelings and my actions". Abusers need to develop empathy for those they are hurting. They are not insecure. They are entitled.

Unhelpful	Helpful
He controls his partner because he's insecure.	He believes he has a right to control his partner.
He needs counselling to deal with his insecurities that cause him to abuse his partner and kids.	He needs access to a perpetrator programme to challenge his beliefs that he is entitled to do what he wants.

---

[17] Bancroft, 2002, 42-44.

But that doesn't make him a bad father.

When a father behaves abusively to the children's mother, that is damaging to the children.[18] Whether the abuser is a biological parent or step-parent, they have a responsibility to support the co-parent. An abuser may use the children to perpetrate abuse; turn a child into an informant, threaten to hurt the child or make the child abuse their mother. The abuser may have reproductively coerced his partner into pregnancy, then using the children from this coercion to control her further. This is brutal and painful. We must be aware of this and not perpetuate the damaging idea that children are not harmed by having an abusive father. Sadly, family courts are often invested in the myth of abusers being good fathers, with women and their children forced into ongoing, dangerous contact with violent men.[19]

Unhelpful	Helpful
He was violent when she was pregnant, but he's never hurt the children.	He was violent when she was pregnant, which makes him a danger to the children and their mother.
Most dads are unfairly treated by the family court system.	Evidence shows that prioritising the fair treatment of fathers in family courts may be detrimental to their children.*
Just because he's abusive to the mother doesn't make him a bad father.	He's abusive to the mother, this results in him being a bad father. A good father respects and values the children's mother.

---

[18] Bancroft, 2002, 235-272.
[19] Harding, 2015. Hill, 2020, 145-175, 241-276.

What about the men?

Women can perpetrate abuse and men can be subjected to abuse. However, when talking about abuse, the gendered nature of it must be acknowledged and not derailed. The vast majority of perpetrators are male (both in heterosexual and same sex relationships). The risks posed by male perpetrators are higher, and are different to those presented by female perpetrators.[20] Overall, language which hides the gendered nature of abuse is unable to effectively communicate the reality of abuse. The reason abusers are more likely to be male is due to male socialisation that insists men have entitlements over women and children.[21] Masculine socialisation leaves men unable to admit weakness and this leads to different challenges when men are subjected to abuse. Men's violence and men's reluctance to admit having been subjected to abuse are rooted in similar issues related to masculinity.

Unhelpful	Helpful
What about men who are abused?	I care about men who are being abuse, so I will take action to support men, and not expect those who specialise in supporting women to do that work.
Women are just as violent as men.	Women are not as violent as men.
Domestic abuse services have to provide support to men.	Domestic abuse services were set up by women to support women. If men need support, they are welcome to develop their own services.

---

[20] ONS, 2020.
[21] Stark, 2009, 105, 155.

Part 3: Her

Why doesn't she leave?

Rather than asking why the abuser doesn't stop his behaviour, very often, the focus will be on the woman, and why she has not left the abuser. By staying with an abusive partner, it is not the woman who is in the wrong; it is her abusive partner who is wrong.

Of women killed by a partner or ex, 37% had separated (or taken steps to separate) from their partner prior to him killing her.[22] Women know that their partner may kill them or their children if they leave. Physiological trauma responses often leave women struggling to leave, while wider societal messages about singleness and a woman's value (particularly if she has children) can cause leaving to seem an unwise decision. Financial need, fear of what he will do to her, immigration status, a desire for the children to have stability and various other factors may also make it hard for her to leave.[23] An abuser's physical violence may leave his partner with brain damage (e.g. through strangulation or causing concussion). This brain injury will impact a woman's ability to leave.[24]

Generally, women do the best they can with what they have and our judgement against her for failing to leave will generally only compound her pain, rather than enabling her to find a way to escape the abuser.

Unhelpful	Helpful
Why doesn't she leave?	Why doesn't he stop?
Why can't she break free of him?	Why doesn't he leave her alone?

---

[22] Allen, Elliot et al., 2020.
[23] Collins, 2019, 102-125.
[24] Nemeth, Mengo, Ramirez et al, 2022. Disabilities Trust, 2022.

Victim. Survivor.

Labelling someone as a victim or survivor may reduce their identity to what was done to them. By focusing solely on the person subjected to abuse, it risks erasing the perpetrator of the abuse, which enables the perpetrator to avoid responsibility for his abusive behaviour. When it is clear that a communication is about abuse, speaking or writing about women, men or people will generally suffice. If someone identifies themselves as either a victim or a survivor, we should listen and support them in how they define their experiences.

Unhelpful	Helpful
She was a victim of sexual violence.	She was subjected to sexual violence.
As a survivor of abuse, she…	As a woman subjected to abuse, she…
Victims often feel ashamed.	People who have been subjected to abuse often feel ashamed.

High risk victim.

The Domestic Abuse Stalking and Harassment Risk Indicator Checklist (DASH RIC) was developed to help police officers, domestic abuse services, and health services decide how dangerous an abuser is and what protection his partner (or ex) needs. As this system has become more widely used, those who are being abused may find themselves categorised according to their partner or ex's risk to them; they become a "high/medium/standard risk victim". However it is the abuser who should be labelled according to his risk, not his partner. A perpetrator can be a high, medium or standard risk, but his partner in herself does not hold any risk. The labelling of women's risk, rather than the perpetrator being labelled can subtly place the responsibility on those who are subjected to abuse and also may mean the level of support a woman can access is not based on her needs, but on her partner/ex.

Unhelpful	Helpful
She's a high risk victim.	He's a high risk perpetrator.
Because of her risk, we should act.	Because of his risk to her, we should take action.

Her Abuser. Her Abuse.

When describing an abuser and/or abuse, it may seem to make sense to describe the abuse as belonging to the person who has been hurt e.g. "her abuser hurt her". However, in doing this, the power dynamics are inverted. The abuser does not belong to the person they hurt, instead the abuser seeks to take ownership of the person they abuse.

Unhelpful	Helpful
Her abuser hurt her badly.	The man who abused her hurt her badly.
She never recovered from her abuse.	She never recovered from the abuse she was subjected to.
Her abuse made her feel ashamed	The abuse she was subjected to left her feeling ashamed

I would never have believed…

When someone tells us about the abuse they have been subjected to, we may respond in a shocked manner, "I would never have believed that you could have gone through something like that." Any expression of disbelief, even when expressed with the intention of empathising with how awful abuse is can be interpreted as, "I don't believe you". By responding calmly and without expressions of disbelief we can support and engage with those who have been hurt in ways that do not reinforce the deep scars of shame an abuser may have left.

Unhelpful	Helpful
Oh my goodness, that's horrific!!!!!	That must have been really tough to tell me. Thank you for trusting me.
I would never have believed it until you told me.	I'm so sorry that they put you through that.

Those women.

There is a common assumption that women who are subjected to abuse are a particular "type" of woman. Images accompanying articles about abuse often portray women cowering in a corner or with a black eye. This reinforces that we would be able to tell by looking at a woman whether or not she is in a relationship with an abuser. This perspective allows us to feel psychologically safe, "If abuse happens to *those* women and I'm not one of *those* women, and no woman I know is, then me and mine are safe from abusers". However, this misunderstanding can prevent women with an abusive partner from recognising he is abusive. It also results in us not recognising if our friend, family member or work colleague is being subjected to abuse.

Unhelpful	Helpful
Those women who get abused.	Women who are subjected to abuse.
Abuse happens to those women.	Some women are subjected to abuse.

It's her low self-esteem.

In order to make it easier to control her, an abuser will seek to reduce his partner's self-esteem. This leads to assumptions that those who are subjected to abuse start off with low self-esteem. This is not the case.[25] An abuser may even deliberately target confident women, in order to tear them down.

It is more comfortable to believe that those with character deficits are the ones subjected to abuse because it allows us to imagine that we are safe from abusers. The logic goes, "If it is done to *those* women then I am safe because I am not one of *those* women." The main difference between someone who was been subjected to abuse and someone who has not is the misfortune of meeting an abuser.

Unhelpful	Helpful
Men who abuse target vulnerable women.	Men who abuse create vulnerabilities in women who may or may not have been vulnerable prior to the relationship.
Women who are abused usually have been abused as children.	Women who are abused have all had the misfortune of meeting an abuser.

---

[25] Stark, 2009, 129.

Getting herself pregnant.

Whether pregnant teenagers or women accused of trapping men through pregnancy, there is predominant idea that women "get themselves pregnant" to trap men. Women cannot get themselves pregnant. They need help to do this. Outside of the very narrow circumstances of IVF and sperm donation; men (and boys) are generally active participants in pregnancy. In reality it is not males who are trapped by pregnancy, but rather women and girls. 40% of women with an abusive partner report that he has coerced them into pregnancy and/or abortion.[26]

Unhelpful	Helpful
Teenage girls get themselves pregnant to get a council house.	Men and boys who impregnate teenage girls should be held accountable for their actions.
Women get themselves pregnant to trap men.	Men impregnate women in order to trap them.

---

[26] Hess and Rosario, 2018.

It's her fault.

Woman blaming is rife in society.[27] Often, when communicating about abuse the focus will be on the woman's actions rather than the abuser's choices. It is our responsibility to ensure our language doesn't reinforce this.

Unhelpful	Helpful
Why doesn't she leave him?	Why doesn't he stop abusing her?
She led him on, he just took her lead. That's not rape.	She chose to interact with him. He chose to rape her.

---

[27] Manne, 2018. Kennedy, 1992. Smith, 2013. Bons Storm, 1996. Herman, 1992. Criado Perez, 2019.

Rescue.

When supporting someone who is being abused, we may feel compelled to rescue them. However, it is not our job to rescue people. Where children are at risk, we have a responsibility to ensure they are safe. However, we need to enable adults to change their own life, not seek to change it for them. Very often we say the opposite to the abuser but then do the same as the abuser. He says, "You have to stay with me." We say, "You have to leave him." It's all focussed on telling her what to do. Instead, we must do the opposite of what the abuser is doing.[28] Where he's disempowering her, we must empower her. When he's isolating her, we must continue to be her friend. When he's reducing her choices, we must show her there are many options.

Unhelpful	Helpful
You have to leave him!	How can I support you?
I'll ring up the helplines and I'll find somewhere for you to live. I'll fix it all.	Can I sit with you while you call a helpline? I'll support you to move forward.
Do you want me to talk to your partner and tell him to stop?	What can I do to help you feel safer?

---

[28] Bancroft, 2002, 372.

That was stupid.

When someone is being subjected to abuse there are various ways they may resist his abuse. They may break the abuser's rules about what is allowed (either overtly or covertly) or they may refuse to do what the abuser wants. The abuser may then increase his abusive behaviour. Friends and family may respond to this by telling the person subjected to abuse that they are stupid and at fault for "causing" the abuser to be violent or abusive.

When someone resists an abuser, this resistance should be honoured not demeaned. In the midst of being highly controlled, they are choosing to take back control and, although we should encourage people to seek safety, we should also recognise that resisting abuse shows that someone still values themselves enough to fight back. As abuse expert Evan Stark explains, women have an "unqualified right to resist" abusive men.[29]

Unhelpful	Helpful
Well, if you didn't do what he wanted, you deserve whatever he did to you.	Well if you didn't do what he wanted, you deserve a medal for standing up to him.
It was so stupid that you stood up to him.	It was so brave that you stood up to him.

---

[29] Stark, 2009, 167.

She is irreparably broken.

While the harm that abusive men cause to women cannot be underestimated, it is crucial that we do not presume that being subject to abuse leaves a woman irreparably broken by what he has done to her. Every woman who has been subjected to abuse will have many strengths and survival skills that enabled her to make it through. The shrinking of women down to what their partner has done to them is demonstrated by the development of "Battered Women's Syndrome" which suggests that when abused, women become "docile, submissive, humble, ingratiating, non-assertive, dependent, quiet, conforming and selfless".[30] This is the way abusers desire their partner to be, it is not a true representation of how women who have been abused behave.

Instead, when we pay attention to women and their stories, we discover the multitude of ways women resist abusers and bravely maintain their autonomy despite the abuser's violence and control.

Unhelpful	Helpful
She let him abuse her.	She will have resisted his abuse.
He destroyed her.	He tried to destroy her.

---

[30] Stark, 2009, 157.

Fell victim to.

By describing a person as "falling victim to abuse/rape", we erase the agency and existence of the perpetrator. A person's choice to rape, sexually violate or abuse another human being is not a hole people fall into, is an active choice made by the abuser which is deeply harmful.

Unhelpful	Helpful
He fell victim to rape.	Someone chose to rape him.
Falling victim to rape is horrific.	Being subjected to rape is horrific.

It's a women's issue.

Often, the subject of abuse is confined to the "women's section" of a newspaper or website, yet abuse is an issue caused by abusers (who are most often men). Content about abusive behaviour and the impact of it should be included in men's media sources. The damage abusers do to women and to wider society should lead to abusive behaviour being categorised as a public health issue. It is something we should all be seeking to understand and address. By making it a "women's issue" we prevent it being taken seriously as an issue for everybody. Even though women are over 50% of the population, when something is deemed a "women's issue" it becomes niche and is treated as a minority problem.

Unhelpful	Helpful
Abuse is a women's issue.	Abuse is the issue of abusers.
Five things women can do to prevent abuse.	Five things men can stop doing that are abusive.

Lived Experience.

The term "lived experience" has become a way of describing the expertise someone may hold based on what they have experienced. The intention in using this term is often to validate such expertise, however the term itself uses two words that mean the same thing (known as a tautology). Can an experience be anything other than lived?

The hope in using this term is perhaps to distinguish experience of abuse that is gained through practice or study about abuse (we could describe this as knowledge about abuse), while experience of abuse gained by being abused by a partner could be accurately described as experience of abuse.

The risk with this term is that it is another way of "othering" those who have been subject to abuse. Personal experience of being abused gives someone expertise in their own experiences of abuse, but does not in and of itself give them authority outside of their own experiences. It is as someone brings their experience into dialogue with knowledge and practice about abuse that they gain authority to speak on abuse more generally.

Unhelpful	Helpful
She is a lived experience expert on abuse.	She is an expert on abuse.
She has lived experience of abuse.	She was subjected to abuse by her ex-partner.

Part 4

Notes

Recommended Reading.

- Out of Control; Couples, conflict, and the capacity for change by Natalie Collins (2019)
- Why Does He Do That? Inside the minds of angry and controlling men by Lundy Bancroft (2002)
- Down Girl; The logic of misogyny by Kate Manne (2018)
- Eve Was Framed; Women and British Justice by Helena Kennedy (1992)
- Misogynies by Joan Smith (1989)
- Trauma and Recovery; The Aftermath of Violence – from Domestic Abuse to Political Terror by Judith Herman, (1992)
- Invisible Women; Exposing data bias in a world designed for men by Caroline Criado Perez (2019)
- The War Against Women by Marilyn French, (1992)
- Coercive Control; The entrapment of women in personal life by Evan Stark (2009)
- Drop the Disorder edited by Jo Watson (2019)
- Anatomy of an Epidemic by Robert Whitakker (2011)
- Delusions of Gender by Cordelia Fine (2011)
- The Gendered Brain by Gina Rippon (2019)
- Pornland; How porn has hijacked our sexuality by Gail Dines (2010)
- The End of Patriarchy by Robert Jensen (2017)

Bibliography

Allen, Rosie Elliot, Katie et al *Femicide Census 2020* Femicide Census (3rd Jun 2022 https://www.femicidecensus.org/wp-content/uploads/2022/02/010998-2020-Femicide-Report_V2.pdf).

Bancroft, Lundy *Why Does He Do That? Inside the minds of angry and controlling men* Berkley Publishing Group, 2002.

Bons Storm, Riet *The Incredible Woman; Listening to women's silences in pastoral care and counseling* Abingdon Press, 1996.

Collins, Natalie *Out of Control; Couples, conflict and the capacity for change*, SPCK, 2019.

Criado Perez Caroline, *Invisible Women; Exposing data bias in a world designed for men*, Vintage, 2019

Crown Prosecution Service, "Revenge Pornography" *Crown Prosecution Service* website (3rd June 2022 https://www.cps.gov.uk/legal-guidance/revenge-pornography-guidelines-prosecuting-offence-disclosing-private-sexual).

Dines, Gail *Pornland; How porn has hijacked our sexuality*, Beacon Press, 2010.

Disabilities Trust, "Making the Link; Female offending and brain injury" *Disabilities Trust*, 2019. (9th June 2022 https://www.thedtgroup.org/media/163444/making-the-link-female-offending-and-brain-injury.pdf).

French, Marilyn *The War Against Women*, Hamish Hamilton, 1992.

Gelfer, Joesph *The Masculinity Conspiracy*, Createspace Independent Publishing, 2011.

Harding, Maebh *How Do County Courts Share the Care of Children Between Parents?* University of Reading in partnership with Nuffield Health, 2015.

Herman, Judith *Trauma and Recovery; The Aftermath of Violence – from Domestic Abuse to Political Terror*, BasicBooks, 1992.

Hess, Cynthia and Del Rosario, Alona *Dreams Deferred: A Survey on the Impact of Intimate Partner Violence on Survivors' Education, Careers, and Economic Security*, Institute for Women's Policy Research, 2018. (2nd June 2022: https://iwpr.org/wp-content/uploads/2020/09/C475_IWPR-Report-Dreams-Deferred.pdf).

Hester, Marianne *Who Does What to Whom? Gender and Domestic Violence Perpetrators*, University of Bristol in association with the Northern Rock Foundation, 2009. (21st May 2024 https://equation.org.uk/wp-content/uploads/2016/02/EQ-LIB-142.pdf).

Hill, Jess *See What You Made Me Do; Power, control and domestic abuse*, C Hurst and Co Ltd, 2020.

Kennedy, Helena *Eve Was Framed; Women and British Justice*, Random House, 1992.

Long, Julia, Wertans, Emily et al, "Femicide census 2009-2018", *Femicide Census*, 2019 (2nd June 2022 https://www.femicidecensus.org/wp-content/uploads/2020/11/Femicide-Census-10-year-report.pdf).

Lorde, Audre. "The Master's Tools Will Never Dismantle the Master's House." 1984. *Sister Outsider: Essays and Speeches*, Crossing Press. 110-114.

Manne, Kate *Down Girl; The Logic of Misogyny,* Penguin Random House, 2018.

Nemeth, Julianna Mengo, Cecilia, Ramirez R et al, "Provider Perceptions and Domestic Violence (DV) Survivor Experiences of Traumatic and Anoxic-Hypoxic Brain Injury: Implications for DV Advocacy Service Provision", *Journal of Aggression, Maltreatment & Trauma*, 2019 (28:6), 744-763 (9th June 2022 https://www.tandfonline.com/doi/abs/10.1080/10926771.2019.1591562).

Okun, Lewis *Woman Abuse; Facts replacing myths*, State University of New York Press, 1986.

Porter, Tony "A Call To Men", Ted website, 2010, (2nd June 2022 https://www.ted.com/talks/tony_porter_a_call_to_men?language=en).

Smith, Joan *Misogynies,* Westbourne Press, 2013.

Stark, Evan *Coercive Control; The entrapment of women in personal life*, Oxford University Press, 2009.

Stockdale, Sue "Words Create Worlds" *Association for Coaching*, no.8 (January 2016), 9-11. (2nd June 2020 https://issuu.com/acglobalcoachingperspectives/docs/january_2016_final/12).

Office for National Statistics "Domestic abuse in England and Wales: year ending March 2016", *Office for National Statistics* website (2nd June 2022: https://www.ons.gov.uk/peoplepopulationandcommunity/crimeandjustice/bulletins/domesticabuseinenglandandwales/yearendingmarch2016).

Office for National Statistics, "Homicide in England and Wales: year ending March 2020" *Office for National Statistics* website (2nd June 2020: https://www.ons.gov.uk/peoplepopulationandcommunity/crimeandjustice/articles/homicideinenglandandwales/yearendingmarch2020).

Oliver, Rhys, Alexander, Barnaby et al. *The economic and social costs of domestic abuse*, Home Office, 2019. (2nd June 2022 https://assets.publishing.service.gov.uk/government/uploads/system/uploads/attachment_data/file/918897/horr107.pdf).

UK Government, "New definition of domestic abuse" *UK Government* website, (2nd June 2022 https://www.gov.uk/government/news/new-definition-of-domestic-violence).

Want to learn more? You could join...

www.ownmylifediscovery.org

www.ingramcontent.com/pod-product-compliance
Lightning Source LLC
LaVergne TN
LVHW072023060526
838200LV00058B/4664